THE
BHAGAVAD-GITA

A BOOK OF HINDU SCRIPTURES
IN THE FORM OF A DIALOGUE
BETWEEN PRINCE ARJUNA
AND THE GOD KRISHNA

THE PETER PAUPER PRESS
MOUNT VERNON • NEW YORK

AN INTRODUCTORY NOTE

THE BHAGAVAD-GITA is a part of orthodox Hindu scripture; it is also a dramatized statement of metaphysics and ethics with strong appeal to the Western world, and in Western eyes it is the most important of all Hindu philosophical and religious books.

The poem was first written probably in the fifth century B.C.; it was presumably reworked many times before reaching its final form in the second century B.C. During its rewritings, it became a vehicle to carry many separate cargoes of theology, ritual, metaphysics and ethics from ancient India — here brought together into one system of belief and practice. Being a synthesis, the book has its paradoxes. But above any paradox it has a single fixed theme: the nature of true Reality or Being — and how man may live in his temporal world and still approach this Eternal Reality.

The background of the book (it is not to be found in the text itself) is the struggle for the succession of the blind king Dhritarashtra. The king has withheld his crown from his oldest son Duryodhana, who is the embodiment of evil, and given it to a younger son who is the embodiment of virtue. But the evil prince has stolen

3

the succession, and all the warriors of the affected tribes have aligned themselves on one side or the other for the battle which will make a final decision between them. This battle is to take place on the plain called the Field of Law, or Righteousness.

The book may be taken literally as a dialogue between the prince Arjuna (on the side of the virtuous succession) and his charioteer the four-armed God Krishna — actually a temporary embodiment of eternal Absolute Being. In such a reading, the incipient battle between the two armies, the last-minute doubts of the warrior-prince as to his right conduct on the battlefield, and the dialogue form of Arjuna's questions and Krishna's answers are all merely devices to dramatize an elaborate ethical and metaphysical exposition.

But the book may be taken also as a great allegory of man's spiritual crisis — and its resolution. The chariot, with Arjuna as the bowman and Krishna as charioteer, is Man. The horses are his senses and passions; the bowman is his active role in life; and the charioteer — the steerer and controller — is his eternal soul — a part of the Universal Soul. This chariot of man is about to enter the battlefield on which only man, among all living beings, is compelled to fight: the Field of Righteousness, or Law.

The battle is between the forces of evil and good, the temporal and the spiritual. Since both good and evil have sprung from the same family roots (or the same individual), the same blood will flow whoever conquers in the battle.

Knowing that his duty as a warrior-prince is to fight for the army of his choice, but sickened by the prospect of killing members of his own family, and his friends; confused by the conflicting claims on his emotions, unable to reconcile his worldly and his spiritual obligations, and fearing too that the forces of evil are invincible, Arjuna, the symbol of Man, falls into a state of helpless emotional paralysis. He is gradually released from this state as his soul, or God (Krishna) who resides in him as a part of the universal Soul, clarifies his understanding and makes his course clear.

After this dialogue (or communion) between God and Man, the man is able to go forward firmly with his worldly duties, even to kill his own kin (or worldly impulses) or to meet inevitable defeat at their hands — because he has learned he can be free of personal or egotistical attachments. With his soul fixed on the Eternal Soul, his body can perform its worldly duties without fear, hesitation, self-seeking or remorse. Thus the Rule of Yoga — the practice of this method of spiritual elevation and fixation — is shown to be the highest way of life, the only way to achieve eventual union with God.

Those who wish detailed guidance through the poem, with the interpretations of the great Hindu commentators, and with many subtleties and references explained, should study the notes and introduction of S. Radhakrishnan's edition, published by Harper's.

The text of the present edition derives from a new version made in 1952 and planned for the general reader. Abridgments have been made to fit the present format — but since the original has much repetition, such abridgments do not spoil the average reader's pleasure or profit.

For the help of the reader: Dhritarashtra is the blind king over whose succession the battle is fought. His charioteer Sanjaya is the narrator, telling the king what has occurred. Duryodhana is the evil elder son who has snatched the succession from its rightful recipient. His army is that of the Kurus, commanded by Bhishma. The forces of good are the Pandus, commanded by Bhima. Arjuna and Krishna are part of the Pandu army.

Both Krishna and Arjuna call each other by many descriptive appellations in the course of their dialogue. But since they speak only to each other, this should cause readers no confusion.

THE GRIEF OF ARJUNA

Dhritarashtra asked: Meeting for battle on the sacred Field of the Law, what did my people and Pandu's people do, O Sanjaya?

Sanjaya replied: King Duryodhana, when he beheld the marshaled host of Pandu's people, went to his master and said: "Look, Master, see this mighty host of Pandu's sons, marshaled by Drupada's son, thy wise disciple. Here are men of valor, mighty archers equal to Bhima and Arjuna in the fray, dread lords, drivers of great chariots.

"And behold also, O noblest of Brahmans, the captains of my host who most excel: yourself, and Bhishma, Karna, Kripa the war-winner, Asvatthaman, Vikarna, and Somadatta's son, also many other mighty men, wielding many sorts of weapons, all right cunning in the fight, who have offered up their lives for me. Commanded by Bhishma, this host of ours is beyond defeat; commanded by Bhima, yonder host can be defeated. So stand you all in due order, each in his place, and guard Bhishma."

The Kuru elder, Bhishma, the grandsire majestic, blew his conch, ringing a high blast of lion-roar, to cheer the prince. Then conches, drums, tambours, gongs, and trumpets straightway struck up; and wild was the sound that rose.

Then Lord Krishna and Pandu's son Arjuna, standing in a great car yoked with white steeds, blew each his glorious conch. Krishna, the High-Haired One, blew *Panchajanya*; and Arjuna blew *God's Gift*. Tiger-Bowel, the doer of grim deeds, blew the great conch *Paundra*. Kunti's son, King Yudhishthira, blew *Eternal-Victory*; Nakula and Sahadeva blew *Sweet-Sound* and *Gem-Blossom*. The Kasi-King, peerless bowman, and Sikhandin lord of the great car; Dhrishtadyumna, Virata, and Satyaki the unconquered; Drupada and Draupadi's sons together, O Lord of Earth, and Subhadra's stout-armed son, each blew his conch.

The wild roar split the hearts of Dhritarashtra's folk, and made the heavens and the earth to ring. Then Arjuna, Lord of the Ape-Banner, seeing Dhritarashtra's folk standing ready, with all weapons set to battle, lifted up his bow, and then, O Lord of the Earth, he spoke these words to Krishna, the High-Haired One, his charioteer: "Drive my chariot, O Courageous One, midway between the two armies, so I may behold those who stand assembled, wishful for battle, with whom I must strive in the toil of war, for I would mark those who are gathered together here eager for fighting, to do the pleasure of Dhritarashtra's evil-minded son."

Sanjaya said: O King, thus bidden by the Wearer of the Hair-Knot, the High-Haired One set the peerless chariot midway between the two armies, before Bhishma, Drono, and all the princes of the earth; and then Krishna spoke: "Behold these Kurus come together, O Pritha's son." There Pritha's son saw assembled fathers, grandsires, teachers, uncles, brethren, sons, grandsons, and comrades, fathers-in-law and friends, in either host. Beholding all these kinfolk arrayed against each other, Arjuna was stricken with a great compassion, and in sorrowful despair he spoke:

Arjuna said: As I look upon all these kinfolk meeting for battle, O Krishna, my limbs grow weak, and my mouth goes dry. Trembling comes upon my body, my hair stands on end;

9

my bow falls from my hand, and my skin burns. I cannot stand in my place; my mind whirls. Unlucky are all the omens that I behold, O Long-Haired One. I see no blessing from the slaying of my own kinfolk in strife; I desire not victory, O Krishna, nor kingship, nor delights. What good to me is kingship, O Lord of the Herds, or pleasure, or life?

Those for whose sake I desired kingship, pleasures, and delights stand here in battle-array, offering up their lives and wealth. Teachers, fathers, sons; and grandsires, uncles, fathers-in-law; grandsons, brothers-in-law, kinsmen too. These though they smite me I would not smite, O Madhu-Slayer, even for the sake of empire over the Three Worlds. Much less for the sake of things of this earth. What pleasure can there be to us, O Troubler of the Folk, from slaughter of our kin? Guilt indeed must lodge with us for doing these to death with our armed hand.

Therefore it is not right that we should slay Dhritarashtra's folk, our kinsmen; for if we do to death our own kin, how can we walk in joy, Madhu Lord? Although these my enemies, whose wits are overthrown by greed, see not the guilt of destroying a family, see not the sin of treason to friends, yet how, O Troubler of the Folk, shall we with clear sight not see the sin of destroying a family? Clearly we must ourselves hold back from this guilt.

Alas, it is a heavy sin we have resolved on, to slay our kin from lust after the sweets of kingship! Far better for me if Dhritarashtra's men, with their armed hand, should slay me in the strife — unresisting and weaponless.

Sanjaya said: So spoke Arjuna, and sank down on the seat of his chariot in the field of war; and he let fall his bow and arrows, for his heart was heavy with sorrow.

THE WAY OF THE RULE

Sanjaya said: Thus was he stricken by pity and despair, with clouded eyes full of tears; and the Slayer of Madhu spoke to him these words:

The Lord spoke: O Arjuna, whence in your

hour of crisis comes this weakness unworthy of your noble race, dishonorable, and contrary to the attainment of heaven? Yield not to unmanliness, O Pritha's son; it is not for you. Cast off this base faintness of heart and rise up, O Terror of the Foe!

Arjuna asked: O Madhu's Slayer, O Smiter of Foes, how can I contend in the strife with my arrows against Bhishma and Drona, who are worthy of my reverence? It were better to live by beggary in this world than to kill such noble masters; were I to slay my masters, all I should enjoy here of wealth and desires would be stained by blood.

We know not which is better for us, that we should overcome them or they should overcome us; before us stand arrayed Dhritarashtra's folk, whom if we slay we shall have no wish to live. My soul stricken with unmanliness, my mind all unsure of the Law, I implore Thee, O Krishna, tell me clearly what will be the better way. I am Thy disciple; teach me, who am come to Thee for refuge. I can see no way to cast out the sorrow that withers my limbs, no, not though I win wide lordship without rival on earth and even to lordship over the gods.

Sanjaya said: So spoke the Wearer of the Hair-Knot, Frightener of Foes, to the High-Haired

One: "I will not make war!" he said to the Lord Krishna, and made an end of speaking. And as he sat despairing between the two hosts, O thou of Bharata's race, the High-Haired One, seeming to smile, spoke these words to him:

The Lord spoke: You have grieved over those for whom grief is unmeet, though you speak words of understanding. But the truly learned grieve not for the dead or the living. Never have I not been, never have you not been, and never have these princes of men not been; and never shall the time come when all of us shall not still be. As the tenant Soul goes through childhood and manhood and old age in this body, so does it pass to other bodies.

He who thinks this Self to be a slayer, and he who thinks this Self to be slain, are both without discernment; the Soul slays not, neither is it slain. It never is born, and never dies, nor may it, being in Being, descend into non-being; this unborn, everlasting, abiding Ancient is not slain when the body is slain. Knowing this Soul to be imperishable, everlasting, unborn, changeless, how can you think, O Arjuna, to slay it or to make it slain?

As a man lays aside outworn garments and takes others that are new, so the Body-Dweller puts away outworn bodies and goes to others

13

that are new. Weapons cannot pierce It, fires cannot burn It, waters cannot wet It, winds cannot dry It. Not to be pierced is This, not to be burned, nor to be wetted, nor likewise to be dried; everlasting is This, dwelling in all things, firm, motionless, everlasting.

Even though you believe It must pass everlastingly through births and everlastingly through deaths, nevertheless, O Strong of Arm, you should not grieve thus. For, to that which is born, the coming of death is certain, and to that which is dead, the coming of new birth is certain. Therefore grieve not over the inevitable. All born things are in their beginnings unshown, in their midway states are shown, and in their endings, O you of Bharata's race, are unshown again; what lament should there be for this?

Looking likewise on your own law, you should not be dismayed; for to a noble warrior there is nothing higher than a righteous war. Happy the noble warriors, O son of Pritha, who find such a war coming unsought to them, as an open door to Paradise.

If you fall in battle, you win Paradise; if you conquer, you have the joys of the earth; therefore rise up resolute for the fray, O son of Kunti. Holding yourself with the same indifference to pleasure and to pain, to gain and loss, conquest and defeat, make yourself ready for the fight; in this way you incur no stain of sin.

Let your reward be in the actions themselves; never in their fruits. So be not moved by the fruits of actions; nor let inaction dwell in you. Abiding under the Rule of Yoga and casting off attachment, O Wealth-Winner, perform your actions, indifferent alike to gain or loss.

Under this Rule of the Understanding a man frees himself even in this life from good deeds and ill. Therefore set yourself to the Rule; skill in actions is the Rule. For under the Rule of the Understanding wise men abandon the fruits of actions, loose themselves from the fetters of birth, and reach that state which is beyond all ill. When your understanding shall have passed through the turmoil of confusion, then alone will you come to indifference as to the things you hear and have heard. When your understanding shall stand firm and moveless in awareness of the eternal Soul, then you will attain the Rule.

Arjuna asked: What are the signs of the man of abiding wisdom who keeps to such awareness, O Long-Haired One?

The Lord spoke: When a man forsakes all the desires that dwell in the mind, O son of Pritha, and is gladdened only in his Soul, and by his

Soul, then he is said to be of abiding wisdom. He whose mind is undismayed in pain, who is freed from longings for pleasure, from whom passion, fear, and wrath have fled, is a man of steady wisdom, a saintly man. He who is free from all attachments and who, whatever fair or foul fortune may come, neither rejoices in it nor loathes it, has wisdom set in permanence.

Let him hold all his senses in restraint, and sit under the Rule, given over to Me; for he who has his senses under his sway has wisdom set in permanence. The man whose thoughts dwell on sense-objects learns attachment to them; from attachment is born love; from love springs wrath. From wrath is confusion born; from confusion wandering of memory; from breaking of memory wreck of understanding; from wreck of understanding a man is lost.

But he who walks among the objects of sense with senses severed from passion and hatred, and obedient to the eternal Self, possesses his Self in due order and comes to clearness of wisdom. In clearness comes freedom from all pains; in those whose minds are free of all pains, understanding is utterly steadfast.

In the unknown night above ordinary mortals the self-subjugated wise man is awake in light; and, knowing his eternal Soul, he sleeps in the dark common daylight of other men. He into whom all desires flow and yet remains unmoved, even as the full immovable ocean is unmoved by entering streams, he alone attains to peace. The man who casts off desire, who moves free of all attachments, with no thought of a "mine" and of an "I," comes unto peace. This is the state of abiding in Brahma, of absolute truth. He that has come therein is never deluded; if even only at his last hours he dwell in it, he passes to oneness in Brahma, the Supreme.

THE WAY OF ACTIONS

Arjuna asked: If Thou declare Understanding to be more excellent than Action, why dost Thou engage me in this grim work, O Long-Haired One? Thou bewilderest my mind with utterance seemingly conflicting; tell me plainly which one way I may win to bliss.

17

The Lord spoke: O sinless one, twofold is the path which I have declared of old. The path of Understanding is for the meditative; the path of Action is for the active. No man can attain freedom from action by abstaining from actions, nor can he become adept in understanding by mere casting-off of actions. For no man ever, even for a moment, rests without action; everyone is compelled to do work by the Moods born of Nature.

From food comes life; from rain comes food; from sacrifice comes rain; and from actions does sacrifice arise. Know that action arises from Brahma; Brahma is born of the Imperishable; therefore Brahma, the everlasting, the all-pervading truth, has his seat in the sacrifice. Thus is the wheel made to revolve, and he who here on earth does not follow its revolving, O son of Pritha, lives in vain, his life being sin and his delight being from the senses.

But for the man whose delight is in the immortal Self, who is contented with the Self, and is glad of the Self, there is nothing for him to work for. He has indeed nothing to gain or lose here either in action or inaction, nor do his purposes depend on people of this earth. Therefore without attachments do the work you have to do; for the man who does his work without attachment wins to the Supreme. For it was with actions that great King Janaka and others came to perfection; you too should do them, for the benefit of mankind. Whatsoever the noble man does, lesser men do the same; whatever he makes his standard, that is the standard the world obeys.

There is nothing in the Three Worlds, O son of Pritha, that I must do; nothing that I have not gotten, or that I shall not get; yet do I continue in work. For if I should not continue ever unwearying in work, O son of Pritha, men would follow My example; these worlds would perish, if I should not do My work; I should make confusion, and bring these living men to harm.

All actions are done by the forces of Nature; but he whose Self is deluded by the thought of an "I" thinks: I am the doer. Surrendering your actions to Me, fixing your mind on the Eternal, cast off all thoughts of the result, forget the "I," and fight.

Arjuna asked: What stirs this man or that to actions of sin, moved even against his will as though by violence, O thou of Vrishni's race?

The Lord spoke: It is desire, it is wrath, sprung from the Fiery Mood, unappeasable in craving, mighty to sin; know this to be the enemy in this world. As fire is enveloped by smoke, as a mirror by dust, as an embryo by a womb, so is this world enveloped by this twin passion. The wisdom of the wise man, O son of Kunti, is surrounded by this everlasting changeling foe, unquenchable and insatiable. The senses, mind, and understanding are said to be its seat; through these it confounds the body's tenant, by enveloping his wisdom.

Therefore, O mightiest of the Bharata race, subdue the sinner, and so loose yourself from this sinful one, destroyer of wisdom and Soul-awareness. The senses, they say, are higher than the limbs; higher than the senses is the mind; higher than the mind is understanding; but higher than understanding is the Eternal Soul. Thus, knowing the Soul to be higher than understanding, and subduing self by Soul, slay, O Mighty-Armed, this changeling foe so hard to reach.

THE WAY OF WISDOM

The Lord spoke: This imperishable Rule I declared to Vivasvat; and Vivasvat declared it to Manu, and Manu to Ikshvaku. Thus was the Rule passed down in order, and kingly sages learned it; but by length of time, O Frightener of the Foe, it has been lost here in the world of men. Now is this ancient Rule declared by Me to you; for you are devoted to Me and are My friend. This is the supreme secret.

Arjuna asked: Near was Thy birth, and far-off was the birth of Vivasvat. How may I know that Thou didst declare it in the beginning?

The Lord spoke: O Arjuna, both you and I have gone through many births. I know them all, but you, O Frightener of the Foe, you know them not. Though birthless and unchanging of essence, and though lord of all born things, yet in My sway over the nature that is My own I come into birth by My own magic. For whensoever virtue fails and lawlessness arises, then, O thou of Bharata's race, do I bring Myself to bodied birth. To guard the righteous, to destroy evil-doers, to establish the law of virtue and religion, I come into birth age after age.

Actions defile Me not; nor have I yearning for the fruits of actions. He who recognizes Me as such is not fettered by actions. Former seekers after deliverance performed their action in this knowledge; therefore do your actions even as the ancients did in former days. What is action, what inaction? As to this, even seers are bewildered. Therefore I will declare to you the knowledge of what is action, that by knowing you can be free of evil.

For of good actions, and of evil actions, and of inaction, there should be knowledge; the nature of action is difficult to comprehend. He who in action comprehends inaction, and in inaction comprehends action, is a man of wisdom; he whose motions are devoid of desire, whose actions are burned clean by the fire of knowledge, is learned.

Free from attachment to the fruit of actions, everlastingly content, unconfined, even though he be engaged in work he does no work at all. Having no desires, his mind under control, his possessions forsworn, performing works through the body's action only, such a one incurs no defilement. Content with what chance brings him, passed beyond the dualities of pleasure and pain, of hot and cold; void of envy, indifferent alike to gain or loss, even in action he remains unfettered. In such a one who, being without attachments, liberated, and possessing a mind established in wisdom, does work as a sacrifice, all work is dissolved.

Brahma, absolute Truth, is the offering; Brahma is the oblation; by Brahma is offered the fire that is Brahma; and to Brahma shall he go who realizes his Eternal Soul in the works that are Brahma. Some there be, men of the Rule, who offer sacrifices to the gods; others in the sacrifice offer their whole actions in the fire which is Brahma. Some offer the ear and other sense-instruments in the fires of constraint; others offer sound and other sense-objects in the fires of the senses. Others offer the workings of all senses and all bodily forces in the fire of self-control, kindled in wisdom.

Others, devotees of breath-control, offer the outgoing breath in the incoming breath, or the incoming breath in the outgoing breath; or they set themselves to restraint by stilling both the outward and the incoming breath. Others, restricting their food, offer the vital functions themselves. All of these, knowers of sacrifice, cleanse their defilements by practice. Feeding on the ambrosial remains of sacrifice, they come to the eternal Brahma. Sacrifices are set forth in the mouth of Brahma. Know that they are all born of actions; so knowing, you may be freed.

There is more bliss in the sacrifice of understanding than in the sacrifice of substance, O Wealth-Winner; and all actions, without exception, O son of Pritha, culminate in understanding. Knowing this, you will never again fall into such bewilderment, O son of Pandu; by this you will see all living beings within your Soul and Self, and likewise within Me.

Even though you are the greatest of sinners, you shall cross the ocean of all evil by the boat of wisdom alone. As a burning fire reduces its fuel to ashes, O Arjuna, so the fire of wisdom reduces all actions into ashes. Nothing else on earth purifies like wisdom; this the adept in the Rule finds in time for himself within himself.

He wins wisdom who has faith, who is devoted, who has mastered the senses; having won wisdom, immediately he comes to supreme peace. He perishes who has neither wisdom nor faith, who is all unbelief; for the doubter there is neither this world nor the world beyond, nor any happiness. But actions fetter him not who has cast off actions under the Rule, who has slain unbelief with wisdom, and who remains in awareness of his immortal Soul. Therefore, O son of Bharata's race, slay the unbelief that remains in your heart with the sword of wisdom, and taking refuge in the Rule, arise!

THE WAY OF RENOUNCING

Arjuna said: Thou tellest, O Krishna, of renunciation of actions, and again of the unselfish performance of actions in the Rule; declare to me surely which of these is the happier.

The Lord spoke: The casting-off of actions and unselfish performance of actions under the Rule both lead to bliss; but of these two ways the unselfish performance of actions is higher than renunciation. He who hates not and desires not is said to have the spirit of renunciation; he is free of pleasure and pain, released from bondage. The ignorant man speaks of renunciation and practice of works as different; not so the wise man. He who applies himself well to one, will pick the fruits of both.

The place which is attained by men of renuncia-

25

tion is reached by men of action too. He who sees that the ways of renunciation and the ways of action are the same, is a true seer. He who is trained in the way of actions, and is pure in soul; he who is victorious over himself and who has conquered the senses; whose soul comes to the Soul of all beings: he is not tainted by works, although he works.

He who is thus united with the Divine Truth will know that he does nothing at all, though seeing, hearing, touching, smelling, tasting, walking, sleeping, breathing; though speaking, emitting, grasping, opening and closing the eyes, for he is aware that only the senses are busy with sense objects. He who does works, surrendering them to Brahma, and releasing all attachment, absorbs no sin, even as a lotus leaf absorbs no water.

Such men of action perform their actions for the purification of their souls; using the body, the mind, the understanding or even the senses, without attachment. Following the Rule, putting aside the fruits of action, they win to fundamental peace; following not the Rule, attached by the workings of desire to the fruits of action, they become bound. When they have cast off by power of mind all works, the Body-Dweller abides in pleasantness and mastery in the nine-gated city of their bodies, neither working nor moving to work.

With understanding set on that Supreme Truth, with the Self at one with That, with heart in That, with That for their whole path, cleansed of defilement by wisdom, they achieve a state of eternal beatitude, never to return here again. The learned see the Eternal equally in a wise and courteous Brahman, a cow, an elephant, a dog, or an outcast man. Those whose minds abide in this equality are victorious over mortality, for Brahma is stainless and equal, and they abide in Brahma.

Unmoved in understanding and unbewildered, the knower of Brahma, who abides in Brahma, will not rejoice when pleasant things befall nor be dismayed at things unpleasant. His spirit unattached to outward touch, he finds pleasantness in his Self; united with Brahma in the Rule, he is fed with bliss undying. For the delights born of touch, having a beginning and an end, are in truth sources of pain, O son of Kunti; the enlightened man has no joy in them. He who has strength to resist the passion of desire and anger here in this life and this body, he is a follower of the Rule, he is a happy man.

The man of the Rule whose joy is within, whose pleasure is within, and whose light is within, becomes Brahma and wins to extinction in Brahma. Holy men whose sins are thus dissolved, whose doubts are thus destroyed, whose ways are disciplined, who delight to do good to all — these achieve beatitude in Brahma. Strict-minded saintly men, who have cast away desire and wrath, and know their Eternal Soul, are enveloped in the blissful extinction of Brahma. Shutting out all external things, concentrating his gaze between the brows, regulating the equality of his in-breathing and his out-breathing, the saintly man who is subdued in sense, mind, and understanding, who has made liberation his supreme goal and is ever void of desire, fear and wrath, is in truth liberated.

Knowing Me to be the receiver and dispenser of sacrifice and austerity, the great lord of all worlds, the friend of all born beings, the saintly man wins to peace.

THE WAY OF MEDITATION

The Lord spoke: He who does his appointed actions without heed to their fruit is both a renouncer of action and a man of the Rule; not he who withdraws, forgoes the sacrificial fire, and performs no rites. Know, O son of Pandu, that what men call renunciation is Yoga, the Rule of disciplined action; for no one becomes a man of the Rule without casting off selfish purposes. Action is said to be the means for the saintly man who seeks to attain Yoga; after he has attained Yoga, serene inactivity is said to be the means. For when one clings not to the objects of the senses and to works, and has cast off all purpose, then he has attained Yoga.

He who is content with wisdom and clear-seeing, who is victorious over the senses, to whom a piece of dirt, a piece of stone, a piece of gold are all equal, is established in the Rule. Most excellent is he whose feeling is equal toward the friend, the lover, the enemy alike; the impartial and the hateful; the stranger and the kinsman; alike to good and evil. Let the man of the Rule hold himself always under the Rule, remaining in seclusion, utterly subdued in mind, without cravings and without possessions.

On a clean spot he shall set for himself a firm seat, neither too high nor too low, and having over it a cloth, a deerskin, and the ritual grasses. On this couch let him seat himself, making his mind one-pointed, controlling mind and sense, and practice the Rule of Yoga to purify his spirit. Let him sit firm, holding body, head, and neck in unmoving equipoise, concentrating his gaze on the end of his nose, with unmoving eyes. Calm of spirit, void of fear, abiding under the vow of chastity, with mind restrained, so let him sit, harmonized, his mind turned to Me and given over wholly to Me. Thus holding himself steadfast under the Rule, the wise man attains the place that ends in extinction, Nirvana, and abides with Me.

The Rule of Yoga is not for him who eats overmuch nor him who eats not at all, O Arjuna; it is not for him who is given to overmuch sleep nor for him who sleeps not at all. The sorrow-slaying Rule is for him whose eating and walking are by rule, whose action in works is by rule, whose sleeping and waking are by rule. When, void of longings and desires, he sets his restrained mind upon his Greater Self, then is he said to be harmonized under the Rule.

A lamp in a windless spot that flickers not; thus is described the man of the Rule who practices union with the Greater Self. When the mind, restrained and concentrated in the Rule, comes to stillness, and when by bringing himself into beholding the Greater Self he has joy in It, and when he knows the infinite bliss that lies beyond the senses and is grasped by the understanding, and in steadfastness swerves not from the Eternal Truth, which having attained, he knows that there is no greater happiness; and where, once established, he cannot be shaken even by the sharpest pain or sorrow; let it be known: this severance from pain and sorrow bears the name of Yoga, the Rule; he must practice this Rule with unwearied mind and labor.

Thus constantly holding the spirit in harmony, the man of the Rule, free of sin, finds easy enjoyment of boundless happiness in touch with Brahma. With spirit following the Rule, with equal vision towards all things, he beholds the Greater Self in all beings and all beings in the Greater Self. When a man sees Me in all things and all things in Me, I am not lost to him nor is he lost to Me. The man of the Rule, who, setting himself to union with Me, worships Me as dwelling in all beings, abides in Me, wheresoever he may abide. O Arjuna, he who sees all things equally in the likeness of the Greater Self, whatever joy or sorrow may betide, he is the supreme man of the Rule.

Arjuna said: Thou hast declared this Rule to

be of even-mindedness, O Madhu-Slayer; but how may it be firmly established, since the mind is so restless and unstable? Restless is the mind, O Krishna, turbulent, forceful, and stubborn; I think it is no more easily to be controlled than is the wind.

The Lord spoke: Doubtless the mind is hard to curb, and fickle, O Mighty-Armed; but by constant practice and dispassion, it may be held. For one who is uncontrolled, I agree the Rule is hard to attain; but by the obedient spirits who will strive for it, it may be won by following the proper way.

Arjuna asked: What of the man possessed of faith, but lacking in self-control, whose mind swerves from the Rule, so that he does not reach perfection in the Rule: to what end comes he, O Krishna? Does he not fall from both paths, and perish like a blown cloud, O Mighty-Armed One, unestablished and bewildered on the road to Brahma? This is my doubt, O Krishna, that Thou must resolve for me; there is no resolver of this doubt beside Thee.

The Lord spoke: Son of Pritha, neither here nor hereafter is there destruction for him; for none who does righteousness comes to evil estate. He who has fallen from the Rule wins to the worlds of those who do godly deeds, and dwells there changeless years; then he is reborn into the house of pure and prosperous folk. There he is given that understanding which he had in his former body, O child of the Kurus, and from this level he strives further for perfection. For he is led onward, without will of his own, by that former striving; if he have even the wish to know the Rule, he passes beyond the mere rituals of worship.

But the man of the Rule who perseveres, when he is cleansed of defilement and brought to perfection through many births, reaches to the supreme goal. Greater than mortifiers of the flesh are the men of the Rule, greater than men of knowledge, and greater than doers of ritual works; therefore O Arjuna, be a man of the Rule. And among all men of the Rule, to Me he is the highest who, with his inner faith absorbed in Me, worships Me with unfailing faith.

THE WAY OF DISCERNMENT

The Lord spoke: Hear, son of Pritha, how if you labor upon the Rule with your mind clinging to Me, and with Me for your dwelling-place, you shall surely know Me in all my fullness. I will tell you of spiritual enlightenment and of discernment, which, if you possess them, there shall remain nothing else to know. Of thousands of men, but few strive to be adepts; of the adepts who strive, few only know Me in verity. My Nature is of eight orders — Earth, Water, Fire, Air, Ether, Mind, Understanding, and Self-Awareness.

This is the lower Nature. But know that I have another and higher Nature than this, one of Elemental Soul, O Mighty-Armed One, and thereby this universe is maintained. Learn, that from these two Natures are sprung all born beings; the source of the whole universe, and its dissolution too, am I. There is nothing higher than I, O Wealth-Winner; this universe is all strung upon Me, as pearls upon a thread. I am the taste in Water, O son of Kunti; I am the radiance in moon and sun, the Word in all the Vedas, sound in the air, manhood in men. The pure scent in earth am I, and the heat in fire; the life in all born beings am I, and the mortification of those who mortify the flesh.

Know Me to be the eternal Seed of all birth, O son of Pritha; I am the understanding of those who understand, the splendor of the splendid. The might of the mighty am I, void of love and passion; and I am the desire which the law bars not, in all born beings.

Know that from Me are the existences alike of the Goodness Mood, the Fiery Mood, and the Darkness Mood; I am not in them, but they are in Me. Bewildered by these three existences of Mood, this world cannot perceive Me, I who am higher than they, and changeless. For this My divine mystery is hard to fathom, but they who make their refuge in Me pass beyond this mystery.

Men of no understanding think I have come from the unshown to the shown state, knowing not that My higher being is changeless, supreme. Veiled by the mystery of My Rule, I am not clarified to all the world; the world is deluded, and recognizes Me not as the unborn immutable. O Arjuna, I know all born beings that have gone before, all that are now, and all that shall be; but Myself, no one knows.

All beings are born to delusion, O you of Bharata's race, Frightener of the Foe, overcome by the duality of desire and hate. But those whose sin is come to an end and who do righteousness are delivered from the delusion of desire and hate, and worship Me, steadfast in their vows. Those who strive for deliverance from age and death and turn to Me, know Me to be the Brahma, the Universal One over Self, and the entire realm of action. Those under the Rule, who know that I encompass the realms of being, and action, and sacrifice, know Me, with their minds at rest, even in the hour of death.

THE NATURE OF BRAHMA

Arjuna said: What is Brahma? What is the Self? What is Action? What is the realm of Things? What is the realm of Gods? Who dwells in our body as the deity of sacrifice, and how does He dwell there, O Destroyer of Madhu? And how mayest Thou be known to us even at the hour of death?

The Lord spoke: Brahma is the Imperishable, the Supreme; the Nature in each of us is called the One over Self; the creative force that makes born beings arise into existence bears the name of Karma. The One over earthly things is mutable Nature; the One over Gods is the Cosmic Spirit; the One over sacrifice is Myself, here in this body, O best of men.

He who at his last hour, when he casts off the body, goes hence remembering Me, goes assuredly into My being. Whatsoever state of being a man remembers at his end in leaving the body, to that same state he goes, O son of Kunti, being absorbed in the thought thereof. Therefore at all times remember Me, and act; if your mind and understanding are devoted to Me, you will assuredly come to Me.

Briefly I will tell you of that state which Veda-knowers call the Imperishable; ascetics void of passion enter this state; and in desire of it men observe chastity and self-control. Closing all doors, shutting the mind within the heart, bringing the life-force into the head, entering the concentration of the Rule, uttering *Om*, the one-syllabled symbol of inexpressible Brahma, and remembering Me — he who does this as he departs, leaves the body and enters the supreme way. Great-souled ones, having reached Me, never again re-enter rebirth, inconstant home of sorrows, for they have reached perfection.

They who know the Day of Brahma to endure for a thousand ages and the Night of Brahma to endure for a thousand ages are true knowers of night and day. At the dawning of this Day all existence springs from the unshown state; and at the falling of this Night it dissolves into the unshown again.

But there is another Existence beyond this, an Unshown beyond this Unshown, an ancient eternal Existence, which is in all born beings, but perishes not with them. This Unshown Being is called "the Imperishable." This, they say, is the Way Supreme, from which, once won, men return not to rebirth; and this is My supreme abode. This is the Supreme Self, wherein all beings abide, wherewith this whole universe is filled; and is to be won, O son of Pritha, by undivided devotion.

Now I will declare the times when the men of the Rule go hence never to return; also the times when, departing, they will come back to rebirth. Fire, light, day, the waxing half of the moon, the six months of the sun's northern course — in these times the knowers of Brahma go hence, and come to Brahma. Smoke, night, the waning half of the moon, the six months of the sun's southern course — in these times the man of the Rule receives the light of the moon, and returns. Light and dark; these are the two everlasting ways of the world; by the one a man never comes back, by the other he returns.

OF THE ROYAL SECRET

The Lord spoke: Now I will declare to you, being without evil thought, this great secret: Knowledge joined with Realization — having which you will be delivered from all evil. This is the king of sciences, king of secrets, the supreme purifier; it is realized by pure perception; it is lawful, easy, changeless.

By My unmanifested form this whole universe is filled; all beings dwell in Me, but I do not dwell in them. And yet the beings do not dwell in Me. Behold My divine mystery. My Spirit which is the source of all beings sustains the beings but does not abide in them. As the mighty winds everlastingly abide in space and go everywhere in space: so do all beings abide in Me.

When an age-cycle dissolves away, O son of Kunti, all beings enter into My Nature; when an age-cycle begins once more, I remould them. Holding Nature under My sway, I remould the whole of this helpless mass of beings again and again, by power of Nature. But these acts of creation and dissolution fetter Me not, O Wealth-Winner, for I remain indifferent and unattached to these acts. Under My control Nature gives birth to all things, moving and unmoving. By this means, O son of Kunti, the world revolves.

The sacrifice am I, and the offering am I, the fathers' oblation am I, the herb am I, the spell am I, the butter-libation am I, the fire am I, the rite of oblation am I; father of this universe am I, mother, sustainer, grandsire, the object of knowledge, the purifier, the syllable *Om*, and the three Vedas; the way, the supporter, the lord, the witness, the dwelling, the refuge, the friend, the origin, the dissolution, the abiding-place, the store-house and the eternal seed. I give heat; I arrest and let loose the rain; I am immortality and death; I am Being and Non-Being, O Arjuna.

O son of Kunti, those who worship other gods and make offerings to them with faith, they too make offerings to Me, though contrary to the true Law. For I alone am the Enjoyer and the Lord of all sacrifice; but since they do not know Me in My true nature, they must fall to the pattern of rebirth. Those whose vows are to the gods go to the gods, those whose vows are to the fathers go to the fathers; those who offer to ghosts go to ghosts; but those who offer to Me go to Me.

When one of earnest spirit sets before Me leaf, flower, fruit, or water, I accept and enjoy this love-offering of the pure in heart. Whatever be your work, your eating, your sacrifice, your gift, your mortification, make it an offering to Me, O son of Kunti. Thus may you be released from the bonds of actions, that bear fruit, fair or foul; your spirit, steadfast in renunciation, shall be delivered and come to Me.

Even those who are lowly born — women, merchants, farmers, and slaves — if they turn to Me, come to the supreme path. How much more easily then, shall righteous Brahmans and kingly sages? Having come into this unstable and joyless world, worship Me. Have your mind on

Me, your devotion toward Me, your sacrifice to Me; do homage to Me. Thus guiding yourself, given over to Me, so shall you come to Me.

THE VISION OF THE GOD

Arjuna said: Out of Thy grace to me hast Thou told the supreme mystic truth of the *One over Self*, whereby my bewilderment is dispelled. For I have heard from Thee in fullness, O Lotus-Eyes, of the birth and the passing away of born beings, and of Thy changeless majesty. Even as Thou hast declared Thyself, so it is. But I wish to look upon Thy sovereign form, O Male Supreme. If Thou thinkest, Lord, that it may be beheld by me, then show me Thy unchanging Self, Sovereign of the Rule.

The Lord spoke: Behold then, O son of Pritha, the hundreds and the thousands of my forms, diverse, divine, various in color and of shape. Behold these celestial ones: Adityas, Vasus, Rudras, Asvins, and Maruts; behold, son of Bharata's race, many marvels never seen before. Behold now, Wearer of the Hair-Knot, the whole universe, moving and still, solely lodged in Me; together with all else that you wish to see. But since you cannot see Me with this your own human eye, I will bestow on you a supernatural eye: behold My divine power.

Sanjaya said: Thus speaking, Krishna, the great Lord of the Rule, O King, then showed to Pritha's son his supreme godly form, of many mouths and eyes, of many marvelous aspects, of many ornaments divine, with uplifted weapons divers and divine; wearing divine flower-chaplets and robes, with anointment of divine perfumes, compounded of all marvels, the boundless god facing all ways at once.

If the light of a thousand suns should suddenly shine in the heavens, it would be like to the light of that mighty being. There the son of Pandu beheld the whole universe, in its manifold diversity, gathered together in one, in the body of the God of all gods. Thereupon the Wealth-Winner, smitten with wonder, with hair standing on end, bowed his head in awe, and with clasped hands spoke to the God.

43

Arjuna spoke: In Thy body, O God, I behold all the gods and hosts of the orders of beings; Lord Brahman sitting on the lotus-throne, and all the saints and heavenly serpents. I behold Thee of many arms, bellies, faces, and eyes, on all sides endless; but I behold in Thee no end nor middle nor beginning, All Sovereign of all forms; I behold Thee bearing diadems, maces, and discs, massed in radiance, on all sides blazing, hardly discernible, dazzling about like fires and suns, immeasurable.

Thou art the Supreme Imperishable, the One to be known; Thou art this universe's ultimate resting-place; Thou art the warder of everlasting Law, Thou art immemorial Being.

Looking upon Thy almighty form of many mouths and eyes, of many arms and thighs and feet, of many bellies, and grim with many teeth, O Mighty-Armed One, the worlds tremble, and I quake. For as I behold Thee touching the heavens, O Vishnu, glittering, many-hued, with yawning mouths, with wide eyes agleam, my heart trembles, and I find neither certainty nor peace. Seeing Thy mouths grim with teeth, fires like the Last Day, I recognize not the quarters of the heavens, and take no joy; Lord of gods, home of the universe, be gracious! These sons of Dhritarashtra, with the hosts of kings, Bhishma, Drona, and the Charioteer's son yonder; likewise the chief of our warriors, hasting enter Thy mouths grim with fangs and terrible; some caught between Thy teeth are seen with heads crushed to dust. As many torrents of rivers flow to meet the sea, so these warriors of the world of mankind rush into Thy blazing mouths. As moths with exceeding speed pass into a lighted fire to perish, so pass the worlds with exceeding speed into Thy mouths to perish.

Thou devourest and lickest up all the worlds around with flaming mouths. Grim glow Thy splendors, O Vishnu, filling the whole universe with fire. Tell me, who art Thou, in this terrible form? Homage to Thee, greatest of gods; be merciful! I wish to know Thee as the first Primal Being, but I understand not Thy ways.

The Lord spoke: I am Time, world-destroying, waxed full and working here to compass the worlds' destruction. Even without thee, none of all these warriors here arrayed in confronting ranks shall live. Therefore rise up and get thee glory; by conquest of your foes enjoy an ample empire. To Me they have already been given in death; you are the mere occasion thereto, O Left-Handed Archer. Then smite Drona, Bhishma, Jayadratha, Karna, and the other mighty men of war: for I have smitten them already.

45

Quail not, but fight; you shall overcome your adversaries in the fray.

Sanjaya said: Having heard these words of the Long-Haired One, Arjuna, trembling, clasped his hands, and prostrating himself, again spoke to Krishna, faltering in voice, and all afraid.

Arjuna spoke: O Long-Haired One, it is right that the world at Thy praise is moved to delight and love; goblins flee in terror on all sides; and all the hosts of the adepts do homage. And why should they not bow to thee, O great-hearted Primeval One, most reverend First Creator, even of Brahma? O boundless Lord of gods, dwelling-place of the universe! Thou art the Imperishable, Thou art Being and Non-Being, the Supreme Verity.

Whatever rude word I have spoken, thinking of Thee as a friend, and hailing Thee through my heedlessness or my affection as "Krishna," "Yadava," or "comrade" in ignorance of this, Thy majesty; and whatever disrespect or jest was shown to Thee, whether alone or with others, playing, lying, sitting, or eating — for these, O Unshakable, Immeasurable, I crave mercy of Thee. Thou art the Father of this moving and unmoving world. Thou art its worshipful and most reverend Teacher. None is equal to Thee; then how should any one excel

46

Thee in all the three worlds, O being of incomparable power?

Therefore with obeisance and prostration I crave grace of Thee, adorable Lord; as father with son, as comrade with comrade, as lover with mistress, bear with me, O God! I am rejoiced to see what none before has seen, but my mind shakes with fear. Show me your old form again: be gracious, O Lord of Gods, home of the universe! I pray to see Thee in the same guise as before, with diadem, with mace, with disc in hand; assume that same four-armed shape, O thousand-armed Universal.

The Lord spoke: In grace, Arjuna, and in divine power, I have shown this supreme form, luminous, universal, boundless, primal, which none save you has yet beheld. Not by the study of Vedas, nor by sacrifices, nor by almsgiving, nor by works, nor by grim mortifications may I be beheld in the world of men in such a form by any but thee, O mightiest of the Kurus. Let not fear or bewilderment be yours seeing this so awful form. With fear cast off, with mind gladdened, behold once more my former shape.

Sanjaya said: Thus having spoken to Arjuna, Krishna once more displayed his own form; the Great-Hearted One, again assuming a pleasant shape, comforted his terror.

Arjuna said: Beholding now Thy pleasant man-like shape, O Troubler of the Folk, I have come to my senses and returned to my natural state.

The Lord spoke: That shape of Mine which you have seen is hard indeed to behold; even the gods are everlastingly eager to behold it. Not for the Vedas, not for mortifications, not for almsgiving, and not for sacrifice may I be seen as you have seen Me. But through un-divided devotion, Arjuna, I may be known, and seen in verity, and entered into, O Frightener of the Foe.

OF THE THREE MOODS

The Lord spoke: Again I will declare the supreme wisdom, highest of wisdom, by understanding which all sages have passed from this life to the highest perfection. Coming unto this knowledge, they become one in quality with Me; they are not disturbed either by creations or dissolutions.

The Great Brahma is a womb for Me; therein I set the seed; thence spring all beings, O Bharata's son. Of all forms arising in all wombs, O son of Kunti, the Great Brahma is the womb and I the father who gives the seed.

O great-armed one, the Moods of *Goodness*, *Fieryness*, and *Darkness*, which arise from Nature, fetter the body's changeless dweller inside the body. Goodness, being pure, is luminous and untroubled, and fetters it by the attachments of pleasantness and of knowledge, O Faultless One. Fieryness in its essence is Passion; being sprung from yearnings and clingings, O sun of Kunti; it fetters the body's dweller with the attachments of action. Darkness, being born of ignorance, bewilders all dwellers of the body; it fetters by heedlessness, sloth, and sleep, O thou of Bharata's race.

Goodness binds to pleasure, Fieryness to action, O Bharata's son; but Darkness, veiling knowledge, binds to heedlessness. When the light of understanding shines forth from all the gates of this body then you may know that Goodness has waxed full. Greed, activity, undertakings, restlessness, yearning; these arise when Fieryness has waxed full, O Bharata-prince. Uncleanness, inaction, carelessness, and confusion arise when Darkness has waxed full, O son of the Kurus.

When after full waxing of Goodness the body-bearer comes to dissolution, he comes to the pure worlds of the most exalted knowers. If in Fieryness he comes to dissolution, he is reborn in men attached to action, and if in Darkness, he is reborn in wombs of dullness.

The fruit of Good actions is pure and goodly; of Fieryness the fruit is pain; of Darkness the fruit is ignorance. From Goodness flows knowledge, from Fieryness flows greed, from Darkness flows heedlessness, bewilderment, and likewise ignorance. Those who dwell in Goodness go up; those who dwell in Fieryness stay in the middle way; those who dwell in Darkness, under the influences of the lowest Mood, go down.

When the wise beholder sees that there is no agent of actions other than the Moods, and sees that which is higher than the Moods, he enters into My existence. Rising beyond these Moods, which are the creatures of the body, the body-dweller, delivered from birth, death, decay, and pain, enjoys immortality.

THE TREE OF LIFE

The Lord spoke: The endless Fig-tree, so they say, has its roots rising aloft and its branches bending down; its leaves are the holy Psalms: he who knows it knows the Vedas. Upward and downward too spread its branches, swollen by the Moods, having sense objects for twigs and buds; the roots stretch downward too, producing works in the world of men.

Its shape is not seen here, nor its extent, nor its beginning, nor its source. When this multiple-rooted Fig-tree has been cut down with the keen axe of unattachment, then may one seek that region whence the knowing ones never will return, saying: we take refuge in that Primal One from Whom streams the ancient cosmic energy. Those who live without pride and bewilder-

51

ment, who are free of the blemishes of attachment, who are constant to the One over self, whose desires are stilled, these are freed from the Pairs called *Pleasure* and *Pain*; these come, unconfounded, to this changeless place. This is My supreme abode, whence men who have come return not; there the sun shines not, neither does the moon, nor fire.

A part of Me has become the timeless Soul in the living world; it draws to itself Nature's five senses and the mind. When this Soul-Sovereign which has been in a body rises thence, He carries with him these five senses and the mind, as the wind carries perfumes from a flower. Presiding over hearing, sight, touch, taste, smell, and mind, He experiences the range of sense.

Whether He rises, or stays, or experiences, the bewildered do not behold Him in this union with the Moods; only those with the vision of knowledge behold Him. Men of the Rule who seek, behold Him lodged in their selves; men of imperfect spirit and vain of mind, although they seek Him, behold Him not.

The radiance in the sun, in the moon, and in fire, that illumines the whole universe: know, this is Mine. Entering the earth, I support all born beings with My energy; as the Soma, the essential sap, I nourish all plants. As the fire of life, I lodge in the bodies of breathing beings; and mingling with the outward and inward breath I digest the four kinds of food. I am seated in the heart of all; from Me comes memory and knowledge, and their loss as well. I am to be known by all the Vedas; I am the framer of the Vedanta, the knower of the Vedas.

Because I am beyond the perishable and likewise beyond the imperishable, therefore in the world and in the books of the Vedas I am called the Supreme One.

He who, free of delusions, knows Me thus as the Supreme One, knows all, and worships Me with all his spirit, O Bharata's son. Such is this most profound teaching that I have told you, O faultless one; understanding this, one becomes a man of understanding and of fulfilled duty.

THE THREEFOLD FAITH

Arjuna asked: What, O Krishna, is the state of those who perform their sacrifices in all faith, but disregard the rules of the Scriptures? Are they in the Mood of Goodness, or Fieryness, or Darkness?

The Lord spoke: Threefold is the faith of body-dwellers; it is born of their natures, of their Moods of Goodness, or of Fieryness, or of Darkness. Hear now about it.

The faith of every one is according to his inherent nature, O descendant of Bharata. Man is composed of faith; he is indeed what his faith is. Men of the Goodness Mood worship the Gods; those of Fieryness worship demi-gods and demons; those of Darkness worship the spirits of the dead, and ghosts. Men who rack themselves with grim mortifications not ordained by the Scriptures, conceited, hypocritical, possessed by the forces of desire and lust, being thoughtless, torturing and oppressing not only their senses but their Body-Dwellers: know these to be demonic in their way.

The sacrifices of the men of Goodness are those observed according to ordinance and offered without desire for any fruit therefrom; their minds are set in certainty, in the knowledge that sacrifice must be done. But know, O noblest of Bharatas, that the sacrifice of the Fiery is offered with a purpose to get fruit therefrom, or for ostentation, or in hypocrisy. The sacrifice of the darkness Mood follows not the rules of the Scriptures, no food is distributed, no hymns are chanted and no fees are paid; it is empty of faith.

Reverence to gods, to twice-born Brahmans, elders and sages; purity, uprightness, chastity, and non-violence: these are called the Mortification of the Body. Speech that gives no pain, that is true, pleasant and wholesome; likewise the regular study of the Scriptures: these are called the Mortification of Speech. Serenity of the mind, pleasantness, silence, self-control, and cleanness of spirit; these are called the Mortification of the Mind.

That gift which is given as a duty, to one who cannot make returns, and with fitness of place, time, and persons, is a gift of the Goodness Mood. But that which is given for the sake of a gift in return, or in hope of reward hereafter, or is grudged in the giving, is a gift of the Fiery Mood. That which is given in an unfit place or time, or to unfit persons, or is given without proper ceremony, or with disdain, is a gift of the Darkness Mood.

THE PATH OF LIBERATION

Arjuna said: I am eager, O Mighty-Armed One, to know the true nature of renunciation and of relinquishment.

The Lord spoke: Putting aside all works done for return is called renunciation; surrender of the fruit of all works is called relinquishment. Some sages say that all action should be renounced as a fault; others say that works of sacrifice, almsgiving, and mortification should not be renounced.

Now hear from Me the true word concerning such renunciation, O best of Bharatas; for renunciation, O tiger among men, has been explained as threefold. Acts of sacrifice, almsgiving, and mortification should not be renounced, but should indeed be performed; sacrifice, alms-

56

giving, and mortification are purifying to the wise. But even these works must be done with relinquishment of attachment and all thought of reward; this, O Son of Pritha, is my final and best word.

To renounce a duty is not right; to renounce it through delusion is a working of the Darkness Mood. To renounce a duty out of fear of its difficulty or painfulness is a renunciation of the Fiery Mood; there is no reward for such renunciation. But to perform a duty merely because it is a duty, without emotional attachment and without thought of reward, is to act from the Goodness Mood. The relinquisher, being enveloped in Goodness, enlightened, and with doubts destroyed, does not hate unpleasant works, and does not become attached to pleasant ones.

Now learn from Me, O Mighty-Armed, the five causes of all actions, as declared in the Vedanta. The body, the self, the senses, the functions, and the fifth of these, Providence: these five are the causes of every action, good or bad, that man sets himself to do, whether with body, or with speech, or with mind.

This being so, he who in imperfect understanding sees his Self alone as the doer, is blinded by his foolishness. He who knows that his Self is not the doer, whose understanding is not defiled, does no slaughter even though he slay these people, nor is he fettered by his act.

The action that is duty, free of attachment, and done without passion or hatred by one seeking no reward, is said to be of the Goodness Mood. But action done by one seeking to gratify his desires, or with thought of "I"; or with great effort, is said to be of the Fiery Mood. The action that is undertaken from bewilderment, without heed to future consequence, destruction, harm, or one's own powers, is said to be of Darkness.

An agent is of Goodness who is free from attachment, speaks not of himself, his constancy, or vigor, and is unmoved by success or failure. An agent is of Fieryness who is passionate, wishful for rewards, greedy; a doer of harm, impure; who is moved by joy and grief. An agent is of Darkness who is unsteady, vulgar, obstinate, deceitful, malicious; who is lazy, despondent and delaying.

Now, O Bharata-prince, hear from Me the three kinds of happiness. First, that happiness wherein a man may rejoice by long practice, and which brings him to the end of sorrow: this, which at first is like poison and in its ripening is like ambrosia, is the pleasure of Goodness, born of the clearness of one's own understanding of the Self. And that which is at first like ambrosia and in its ripening like poison, which comes from union of the senses with the objects of their desire, is the pleasure of Fieryness. That pleasure which begins and ends in self-delusion, which comes from sleep, indolence, and self-deception, is the pleasure of Darkness.

There is not, either on earth or in heaven among the gods, anything that is free from these three Nature-born Moods. The works of Brahmans, lords, men of affairs and serfs, O Frightener of the Foe, are different from each other by virtue of the different Moods by which they spring from Nature.

Restraint of mind and senses, austerity, purity, patience, uprightness, knowledge, discernment, and faith in God, are the natural duties of the Brahman, born in him. Bravery, heroic temper, steadiness, skill; not fleeing in battle, generosity and princeliness are the natural duties of the lord. Tilling the ground, herding cattle, and trading are the natural duties of practical men of affairs; and the natural duty of the serf is service.

Only as each man devotes himself to his own proper duty does he attain to consummation. Hear how by devotion to his proper duty he wins consummation. A man wins consummation by worshiping, with his proper work and duty, Him who pervades the universe and is the source of all. There is more happiness in following one's own duty without skill, than in doing another's duty well. To do the work assigned by Nature incurs no sin. No one should forsake the work to which he is born, even though it is faulty; for all undertakings are clouded by faults as fire is by smoke.

He whose understanding is without attachment, who has wholly conquered self, and who is freed of desires, wins, by this relinquishment, the supreme consummation.

Learn from Me briefly, O son of Kunti, how he who has won such consummation wins to Brahma, the highest goal of knowledge. Possessed of purified understanding, restraining self by firmness, relinquishing sweet sound and all other objects of the senses; casting aside passion and hatred, living alone away from men, eating little, restraining speech, body, and mind, given over to the Rule of meditation, turned everlastingly to passionlessness, free from egotism, from force, pride, desire, wrath, and possession, without thought of a "mine," and at peace, one becomes fit for Brahmahood.

Becoming Brahma, he is clear of spirit, he grieves

not and desires not; indifferent toward all earthly beings, he wins to supreme devotion to Me. By devotion he recognizes Who and What I am; thus knowing Me in verity, he speedily enters into Me. Even though he is a doer of many works, by taking refuge in Me he attains by My grace to the eternal changeless home.

Arjuna spoke: My bewilderment has vanished; I have regained understanding by Thy grace, O Never-Falling. I stand free from doubt. I will do Thy word.

Sanjaya spoke: Thus did I hear this wondrous, hair-stirring dialogue of Krishna and the great-hearted son of Pritha. By the grace of Vyasa I heard this supreme secret from Krishna, the Lord of the Rule, himself reciting his Rule.

O king, each time I remember this wondrous and holy dialogue of the Long-Haired One and Arjuna, I rejoice again. And each time I remember the exceedingly wondrous form of the Lord, great astonishment comes upon me, O king, and I rejoice again. Wherever Krishna is, the Lord of the Rule; wherever the archer is, Pritha's son, there, I know, are fortune, victory, welfare and good life.